THE

BIKE

REPAIR BOOK

THE
BIKE REPAIR
BOOK

THE HANDY GUIDE TO BICYCLE MAINTENANCE

Hardie Grant

QUADRILLE

THE CITY BIKE

When I think of a city bike, I think of Rutger Hauer weaving through the centre of Amsterdam with Monique van de Ven on the back. If you're not familiar with the film *Turkish Delight*, think of a romantic version of the swap-bike, but with a sturdy rear end so you can carry your beloved with you. In essence, a basic bike.

City bikes are the house sparrows of bikes. They are so ordinary that I no longer notice them, but if I had to draw one, I'd find it difficult. But just like house sparrows, bikes are special, if you look closely at them.

I must be honest and admit that I've always treated my bikes badly. I've done some bad things. I've left bikes behind in the city just because the tyre was flat. I've left them in places where they are not allowed, just so the authorities would take them away. Some of them I just never collected. But I wasn't brought up like that. My father had a deep respect for bikes. Squealing tyres or crunching gears were ear-splitting to him. He repaired bikes for me and my children. He taught me how to fix a tyre. He taught my children how to cycle. He passed away this year. He left behind a plastic crate, containing all the tools needed to repair a bike.

It was just before he died that I had the idea to write this book. I bought a decent city bike from an artisan bicycle maker (Da Vietsie in Amersfoort), a Rutger Hauer bike, and resolved finally to look after this bike. But how to do so?

I delved into books and went to bike mechanics for advice, to learn the basic tricks of the trade. The result is this book, intended for anyone who has always treated their bike badly, but wants to improve their life. It's for parents who want to learn to repair small faults with their children's bikes. And it is also a book for myself. So I can repair my mother's bike.

GERARD JANSSEN

CONTENTS

THE EVOLUTION OF THE BICYCLE

BIKES ARE STRANGE METAL WORKS OF ART WITH WONDERFUL COMPONENTS: BEARINGS, SPOKES, CHAINS. A TRUE CITY BIKE IS THEREFORE NOT A RESULT OF DESIGN, BUT AN EVOLUTION.

The ordinary city bike is a form of perfection. In 2007 the Delft cycling professor Arend Schwab and his colleagues wrote a groundbreaking article on the stability of the bicycle. Until that point, the reason why bikes are so stable when moving was not truly understood. The theory was that it had something to do with the gyroscopic effect of the rotating wheels. But it appears to have much more to do with the subtle interplay between frame and handlebars, an interplay that was discovered through falling and standing up. 'I don't think that we could have improved the design of the city bike through science,' said Schwab. It's a sort of perfection that no person can oversee, perfection that is the result of adaptation – and of a few good ideas, such as the bicycle chain. At first, bicycles came with a huge front wheel, with the pedals connected directly to the wheel. Then some genius came up with the idea to use chains and sprockets, so that the pedals could be freed from the wheel.

1861: THE PEDALS

In 1861, Parisian Ernest Michaux built a bicycle with pedals on the axle of the front wheel: a velocipede. This led to the 'penny farthing', a bicycle with a huge front wheel. The bigger the front wheel, the greater the distance the cyclist can travel with just one pedal movement, but the more difficult it is to climb onto the bike.

1816: THE ROTATABLE FRONT FORK

German Carl Ludwig Christian, the Free Lord of Drais von Sauerbronn, designed the draisine, an improved version of the hobby horse, that had been around for some time. The most significant improvement was the rotatable front fork, which made the hobby horse steerable.

1885: THE BICYCLE CHAIN

James Starley and his nephew John Kemp Starley built the first so-called 'safety bike'. The wheels were both the same size, and the saddle was placed above the centre of gravity. The pedals were separated from the wheels and the rotating movement was transmitted to the rear wheel via a chain and gears.

1930: THE GEARS

During the 1930s, the first derailleur systems appeared in Italy. The derailleur system on a bike ensures that the chain can move from one gear to another so that pedalling becomes harder or easier. From the 1960s onwards, gears have been used on most bikes. Before then, they were mainly used on racing bikes.

PART 1

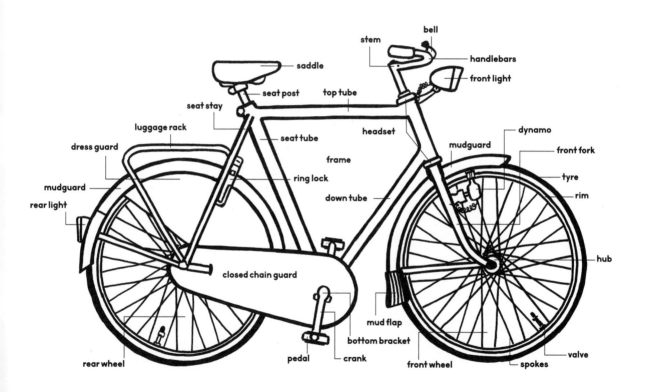

saddle

bell

stem

handlebars

front light

seat post

top tube

seat stay

headset

luggage rack

dynamo

mudguard

dress guard

seat tube

front fork

frame

tyre

mudguard

ring lock

rim

rear light

down tube

closed chain guard

hub

mud flap

rear wheel

pedal

crank

bottom bracket

front wheel

valve

spokes

THE ANATOMY OF THE BIKE

FRAME

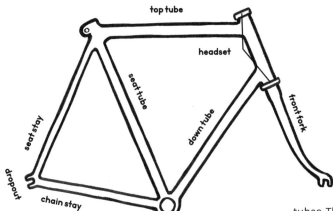

top tube

headset

seat tube

down tube

front fork

seat stay

dropout

chain stay

bracket

The frame is the spine of the bicycle, usually made of metal tubes. A frame consists of two parts. The front frame consists of an upper tube, a down tube, a seat tube and a headset tube, into which the handlebars fit. The rear frame is made of thinner tubes. This is the triangular structure in which the rear wheel sits. A nice old-fashioned bike has a frame that you can dismantle. Newer bikes usually have a one-piece frame. Modern, expensive bikes often have thick tubes, so they look robust and rugged, but this is just for show. Frames with thinner tubes can also be strong. A frame almost never needs to be repaired.

WHEELS

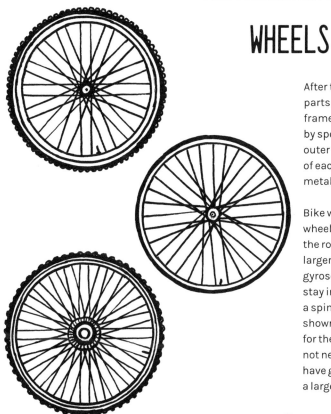

After the frame, the wheels are the most important parts of a bike. They are much more vulnerable than a frame. A bike wheel consists of a rim that is attached by spokes to a hub, which is a double cylinder. The outer and inner cylinders can rotate independently of each other. This is possible because tiny, round metal balls – the ball bearings – move around inside.

Bike wheels come in various sizes. The bigger the wheel, the less nuisance you suffer from bumps in the road. It has long been thought that a bike with larger wheels is more stable, due to the so-called gyroscopic effect: something that rotates wants to stay in its own plane (the same effect ensures that a spinning top does not fall over). But research has shown that this gyroscopic effect is not so important for the stability of a bike. Large wheels are therefore not necessary, especially if the road is flat, and you have good cycle paths. The further disadvantage of a large wheel is that it buckles more easily.

RIM

A rim is made of steel, aluminium or – on older bikes – chrome. The rim is U-shaped, so the tyre can rest inside it. Some rims are suitable for a so-called clincher tyre: an 'ordinary' external tyre, with two internal steel wires that ensure the tyre grips the rim firmly. Racing bikes often have rims with a shallow bed, suitable for tubes, which are racing bike tyres without a steel wire. Tubes can be inflated more and ensure lower rolling resistance.

SPOKES

Most wheels have 36 spokes, although this can also be 32, 28 or 24. The more spokes, the stronger the wheel, but also the heavier the bike. Attaching spokes is called braiding or lacing. There are various 'spoke patterns' in which you can arrange spokes in a wheel, such as the 1-over-4 spoke pattern, the 1-over-3 spoke pattern and the 1-over-2 spoke pattern.

It appears logical to insert the spokes directly from the centre outwards, so directly from the hub to the rim. This 'radial' spoke pattern was common in the earliest bikes; however, when braking and driving the wheel, the forces are not transferred properly. Due to the flexibility of the spokes, the hub is able to turn slightly without the rim also turning. This does not happen if the spokes are crossed.

HUB

The last component of the wheel is the hub. In its simplest form, the hub consists of an axle, ball bearings and a hub body. The ball bearings allow the hub body – a metal cylinder – to rotate while the axis is still. The hub body is usually made of aluminium.

The ball bearings must be lubricated with a small amount of grease, in order to be able to do their job properly. The hub flange is the name of the upright edge of the hub body, which contains the holes for the spokes.

HANDLEBARS

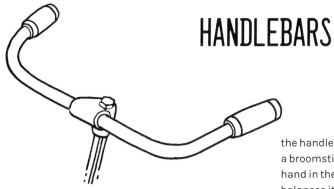

Most city bikes have upright handlebars. It's best when the handlebars are as wide as the rider's chest. But there are no fixed rules. If you want to, you can fit huge clown handlebars to your bike, and ride around like a cool motorcyclist.

The handlebar system consists of an upper tube, the handlebars and the headset. The handlebars are not only important for steering but also for maintaining balance. The stability of a good bike has a lot to do with the interaction between the frame and the handlebars. It's a bit like how you can balance a broomstick on one flat hand, by moving your hand in the direction the broomstick falls. A bike balances itself in exactly the same way, because the handlebars 'fall quicker' than the frame. As a result of this falling motion, the frame is pulled back upwards. If you give your bike a push and run alongside it, and give the bike a soft tap, you will see how it works and that the bike will right itself.

If you've lost the thread here, it doesn't matter. What is important is that you understand that a fully loaded basket on the front of the bike, or a jacket on your handlebars will make the bike a little less stable, because the interaction between the frame and the handlebars is disrupted.

SADDLE

A saddle consists of two components: the saddle itself and a saddle strap that attaches the saddle to the seat post. The seat post is the rod that is inserted in the frame. Sometimes, on older bikes, it becomes rusted solid. This is something to watch out for when purchasing a second-hand bike. On newer bikes, the saddle and saddle strap are integrated.

CHAIN

One of the greatest breakthroughs in the evolution of the bicycle was the invention of the bicycle chain, which enables the pedals to be separated from the wheels and – in conjunction with the gears – allows the pedals to rotate at a different speed to the wheels.

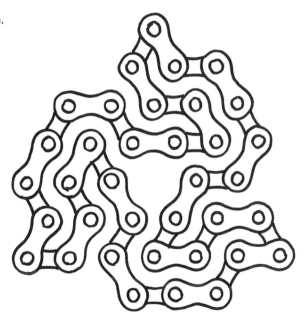

BRAKES

BACK-PEDAL BRAKE

The back-pedal brake is only really found in the Netherlands. Advantages of the back-pedal brake are that it doesn't break very easily and that it requires little maintenance. One disadvantage is that in hilly areas, a back-pedal brake can overheat if you brake hard and often during a descent.

The back-pedal brake is located in the hub of the rear wheel, the hub brake. Inside the hub, there is a screw thread, which pushes up a wedge-shaped disc when you back pedal, so that pieces of metal are pushed out from inside the hub against the hub cylinder. A piece of metal is pushed out from inside the hub against the rotating cylinder and the wheel comes to a standstill.

The advantage of a back-pedal brake is that all of the components are contained within the rear hub and are protected against wind and rain.

Another advantage is that you can cycle and brake without using your hands. (But that can also be a disadvantage, if you actually do it.)

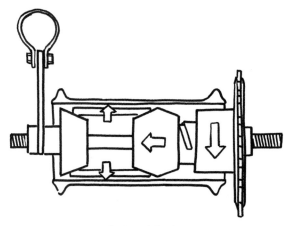

back-pedal brake

RIM BRAKE

This is the familiar hand brake with the rubber brake blocks that press on the rim when you pull the levers on the handlebars. They work well in dry weather, but not so well in wet weather.

DISC BRAKE

The disc brake works in the same way as the rim brake, except that the blocks press against a flat, round disc attached to the hub, rather than on the rims.

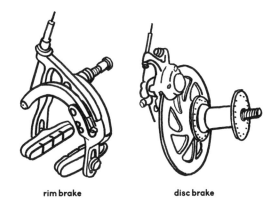

rim brake   disc brake

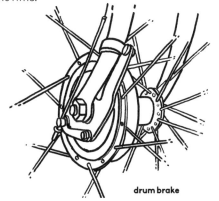

drum brake

DRUM BRAKE

The principle of the drum brake is similar to that of the hub brake. It is operated by a lever on the outside of the hub. You operate this via a brake cable, which again presses metal against the inside of the hub and the bike comes to a standstill. Drum brakes are located in both the front and rear wheel. It is a sort of double reverse pedal brake that you operate with the levers on your handlebars.

GEARS

GEAR HUB

Just as there are hubs in which a brake is housed, there are also hubs in which ingenious 'planetary gear systems' are concealed, which ensure that you can use different gears on a bike. By combining larger and smaller gears, you can drive the wheels at different speeds from those at which you are pedalling. A gear hub is complicated, and dismantling and repairing such a hub is an advanced bike-maintenance art.

DERAILLEUR

A derailleur is the worm-shaped gear attachment that you will see hanging from the rear wheel of a racing bike. The Dutch word is 'kettingwielversteller'. Bikes with a derailleur do not have a (closed) chain guard, and when changing gear, the chain moves from one cog to another, so that you can pedal lighter or harder.

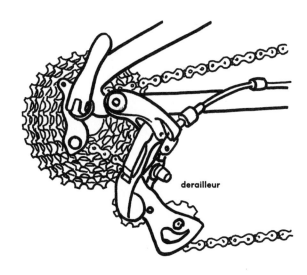

derailleur

CRANK

The crank is the metal shaft between the bottom bracket and the pedal. The bottom bracket, the cranks and the cog together are called the crank set.

PEDALS

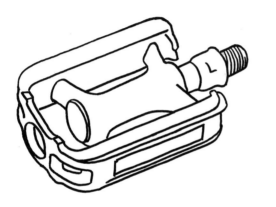
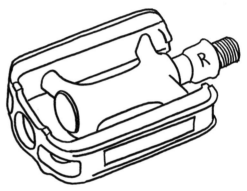

Pedals look a bit like a hub. They also contain ball bearings that ensure that the pedals can rotate around their axle while the pin to which they are attached does not. The left pedal has an anticlockwise screw thread and the right pedal a 'normal' clockwise screw thread.

MUDGUARD

A mudguard ensures that no mud or water splashes onto your clothes, and vice versa it also protects the bike. Most mudguards have to be screwed in place, but there are also some that you can attach with clips and elastic. For racing cyclists there are also so-called 'ass savers', which you clip beneath your saddle. The discovery was made by a Swede who stuck a piece of cardboard under his saddle to protect his behind and was surprised by the good result. Perhaps an idea if you are fed up of those rattling mudguards.

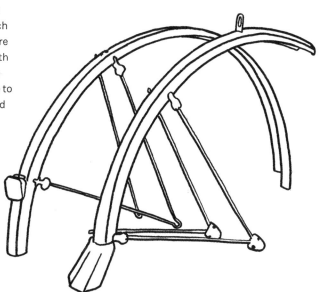

LUGGAGE RACK

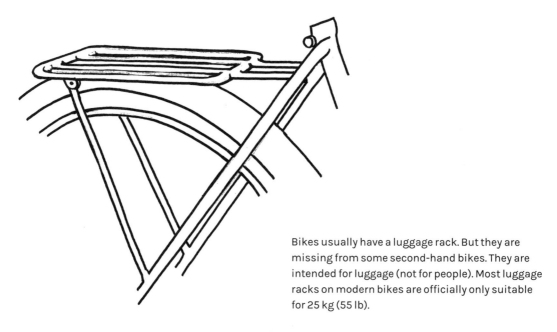

Bikes usually have a luggage rack. But they are missing from some second-hand bikes. They are intended for luggage (not for people). Most luggage racks on modern bikes are officially only suitable for 25 kg (55 lb).

LIGHTS

Older bikes are often fitted with a dynamo. The impeller of the dynamo touches the side of the tyre. As the wheels rotate, this turns a magnet in the dynamo, which generates electricity. An alternative to this – found on newer bikes – is the hub dynamo. This dynamo works on the same principle, only the energy is generated by the hub and not by the tyre. If you don't have a dynamo, you can always use lighting that runs on batteries.

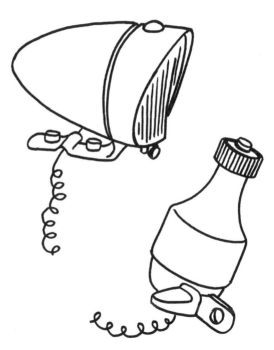

PART 2

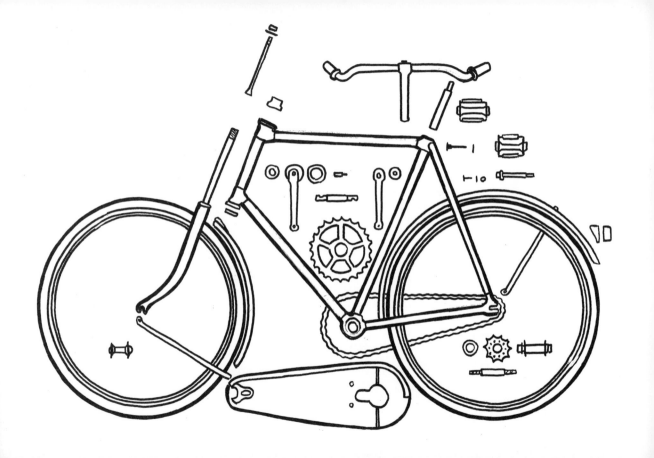

THE WORKSHOP

I have always had a love-hate relationship with bike mechanics. They are always very precise and well-organized, but just quickly repairing a puncture is out of the question. Before anything happens, everything must be tidied up and all the tools laid out. I'm not like that at all. I get started, only to discover that there are no puncture repair patches to hand, or that there is no rubber solution left, or that I need a spanner. Sometimes I can walk back and forth seven times before I have the correct-sized spanner or Allen wrench/key. And so often, the exact size that I need is missing, because I didn't tidy my tools away properly last time. If I go to the bike shop to buy something I need to repair my bike, I often have to go several times, because I hadn't thought about exactly what I needed, or I forgot to make a note of a size. The writer Simon Carmiggelt once said: 'Teetotallers are right, but only alcoholics know why.' It's the same with organized working: the perfectionists are right, but only the scatterbrains know why.

One principle behind the creation of this book was: 'If you can't repair it, you don't really own it.' I had to take a bike completely to pieces, only to find out that I couldn't put it back together properly. Bikes are a lot more complex than you think, and ironically, ordinary common or garden bikes are more complex than designer or racing bikes. The latter are often specifically designed to be quick and easy to repair.

A good bike mechanic is a craftsman. It's a long road to becoming a good one, but it's not difficult to take the first few steps.

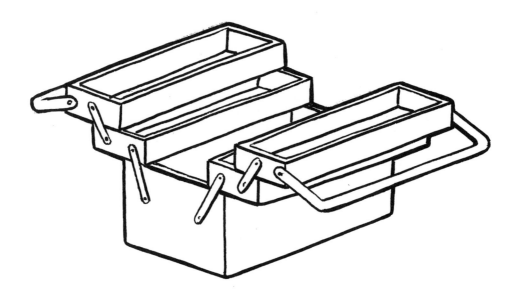

BIKE TOOLS

A BIKE SURGEON HAS A SPECIAL TOOL CHEST, CONTAINING SOME CURIOUS TORTURE INSTRUMENTS. YOU DON'T NEED TO BUY ALL OF THESE THINGS, BUT THEY ARE HANDY. I ONCE MET A CLEVER CHAP, WHO ALWAYS BOUGHT THE CHEAPEST TOOL KIT FIRST. IF A TOOL BROKE BECAUSE HE USED IT A LOT, HE WOULD THEN BUY A MORE EXPENSIVE VERSION OF THAT TOOL.

SPOKE SPANNER

CASSETTE REMOVAL TOOL/ CHAIN WRENCH

YOU CAN USE THIS TO TIGHTEN
OR LOOSEN THE SPOKES.

A HANDY TOOL IF YOU HAVE A SPORTY
BIKE WITH A DERAILLEUR.

SPANNER

RING SPANNER

AN ESSENTIAL TOOL (THE SIZE YOU NEED IS ALWAYS MISSING FROM YOUR KIT). FOR A BIKE, YOU OFTEN NEED SPANNER SIZE 10 OR 15.

A RING SPANNER IS A TYPE OF SPANNER, BUT WITH A RING-SHAPED 'MOUTH'.

SOCKET SPANNER

HEXAGONAL WRENCHES/ ALLEN KEYS

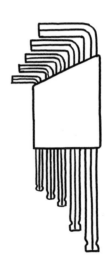

THE SOCKET SPANNER HAS HEAD
ATTACHMENTS IN VARIOUS SIZES.

HEXAGONAL WRENCH SIZE 5 IS THE MOST COMMONLY
USED, CERTAINLY FOR MODERN BIKES.

BICYCLE PUMP

TYRE LEVERS

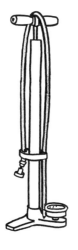

IT'S A GOOD IDEA TO BUY A BICYCLE PUMP WITH A
PRESSURE GAUGE. THE MAXIMUM PRESSURE IS STATED
ON THE OUTER TYRE. FOR AN ORDINARY CITY BIKE
THIS IS USUALLY BETWEEN 2 AND 3 BAR. A BIKE WITH
CORRECTLY INFLATED TYRES RIDES MUCH BETTER.

YOU CAN USE THESE TO
LEVER THE OUTER TYRE FROM THE WHEEL.

SCREWDRIVERS

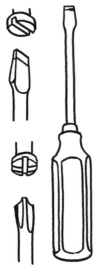

A 'NORMAL' OR FLAT-HEAD SCREWDRIVER AND A
CROSS-HEAD SCREWDRIVER ALWAYS COME IN HANDY.

BOLT SPANNER

HAS A SLIGHTLY LONGER ARM, WHICH MAKES IT EASIER
TO APPLY FORCE THAN WITH AN ORDINARY SPANNER.

PEDAL SPANNER

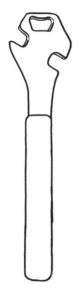

JUST SLIGHTLY NARROWER THAN AN ORDINARY
SPANNER, SO IT'S PERFECT FOR USE ON
PEDALS AND HUBS.

CONE SPANNER

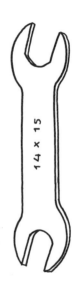

14 x 15

SIMILAR TO THE PEDAL SPANNER.

HEADSET BOLT SPANNER

CRANK PULLER

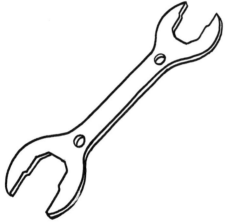

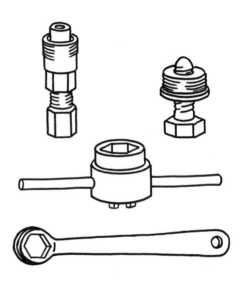

ORDINARY SPANNERS ARE NOT USUALLY BIG ENOUGH
FOR THE HEADSET BOLT. THIS SPANNER IS A BIT MORE
USEFUL THAN TONGUE-AND-GROOVE PLIERS.

THE PERFECT (AND ESSENTIAL) TOOL FOR FITTING OR
REMOVING A SPLINELESS CRANK (SEE PAGE 78).

CHAIN TOOL

WIRE CUTTERS

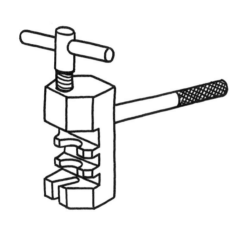

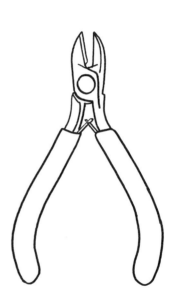

A SPECIAL TOOL FOR REMOVING LINKS FROM CHAINS.

FOR CLIPPING BRAKE CABLES.

BOLT PLIERS

TONGUE-AND-GROOVE PLIERS

**USEFUL FOR LOOSENING
STUBBORN NUTS.**

**USEFUL FOR LOOSENING
STUBBORN NUTS.**

WHEEL STRAIGHTENER

FORK SPREADER

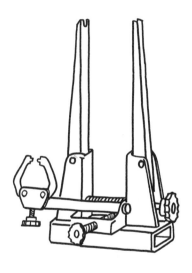

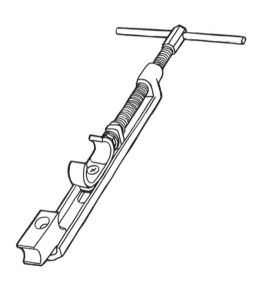

YOU TURN A WHEEL IN THIS TO CHECK
IF IT HAS A BUCKLE IN IT.

A FORK SPREADER MAKES IT EASIER TO REMOVE
YOUR REAR WHEEL FROM YOUR BIKE.

CLOTH

YOU GET YOUR HANDS DIRTY WHEN YOU WORK ON A BIKE. IF YOU DON'T LIKE GETTING YOUR HANDS DIRTY, YOU CAN USE MECHANICS' GLOVES. A CLOTH THAT IS OK TO GET DIRTY IS ALWAYS USEFUL.

SOLUTION

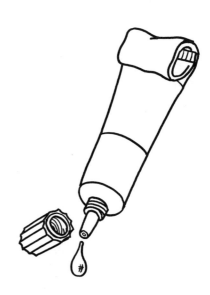

THIS IS THE WORD FOR PUNCTURE REPAIR ADHESIVE.

SPRAY LUBRICANT

ABRASIVE PAPER

**WD-40 OR ANOTHER BRAND OF
PENETRATING OIL.**

**TO ROUGHEN THE INNER TUBE IN THE
AREA OF ANY REPAIR PATCHES.**

PATCHES

BIKE LIFT

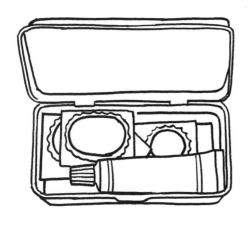

YOU CAN MAKE THESE YOURSELF
FROM AN OLD INNER TUBE.

WITH A BIKE LIFT YOU CAN SUSPEND THE BIKE FROM
THE CEILING AND WORK AT EYE LEVEL.

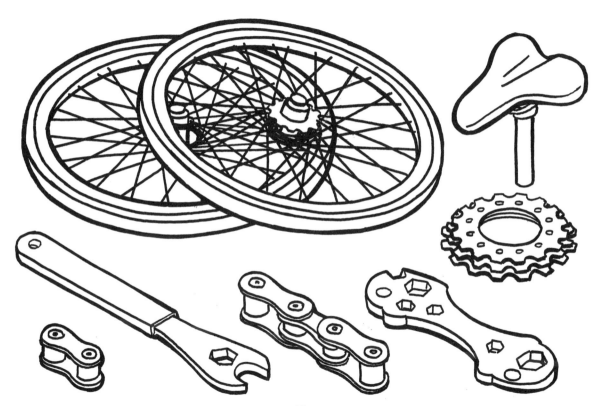

PART 3

BIKE REPAIR

ON THE FOLLOWING PAGES YOU WILL FIND MORE INFORMATION ON EACH
BIKE COMPONENT AND HOW TO REPAIR IT IF SOMETHING BREAKS.

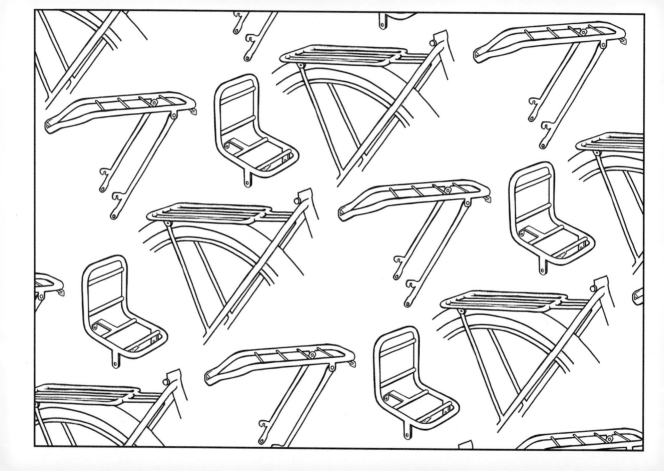

LUGGAGE RACK

Every Dutch person knows how to jump on the back of a bike. You take a little run-up, give the rider a little shove and then do a sort of triple jump, after which you land – usually sidesaddle – on the luggage rack. It isn't particularly comfortable, but sometimes it is handy. Or romantic. Everyone knows what it's like to have someone on the back. The world becomes heavy and syrupy, as if you're cycling underwater.

What few people know is that luggage racks are not intended to have someone sitting on them at the back. Most luggage racks on modern bikes are officially only suitable for 25 kg (55 lb). It is what a designer might call a design fault: something the size of your behind, which invites you to sit on it, but on which you are not allowed to sit. Although from experience you know that you can sit on the back of most city bikes, if you want to be certain, there are some bikes that guarantee up to 80 kg (176 lb).

STEP-BY-STEP INSTRUCTIONS

REPLACING THE LUGGAGE RACK

1. Remove the lock.

2. Loosen the two bolts that are used to attach the luggage rack to the frame.

3. Loosen a wheel nut to release one side of the luggage rack. It is best to do this one by one and immediately re-tighten the wheel nut. This is so that the wheel remains upright in the frame and the chains stay under tension.

4. Repeat on the other side.

5. The new luggage rack can now be fitted. Repeat the above in reverse order. Once again, nut by nut, so that the wheel remains upright.

6. Attach the luggage rack to the frame with the bolts. Fit the lock.

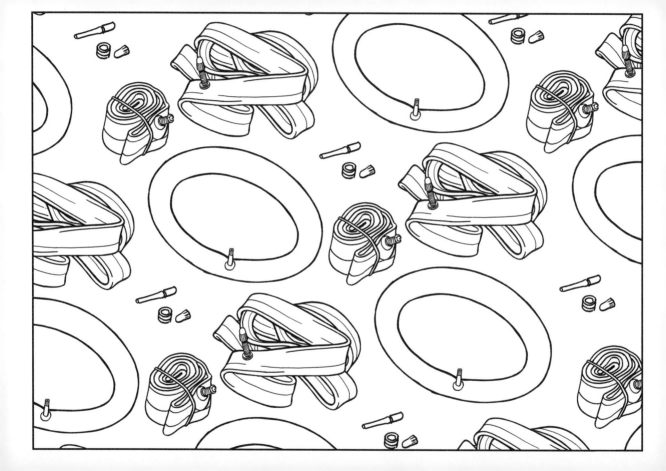

TYRES

Repairing a tyre is like pricking a pea with your fork: it looks easy, but it often goes wrong. At first sight, it appears simple – whip off the tyre, take out the inner tube, find the hole, patch it and put it all back together. But there is the evil tyre repair ghost to contend with, who makes sure that the glue is dried up or there are no patches left, or that there is another hole in the inner tube.

Simply turning a bike upside down is more difficult than it looks. Especially with the baskets and grills that many bikes have these days. Before you know it, you have an ugly, bruised finger. It is for a good reason that bike mechanics hang bikes on a so-called bike lift (see tools page 50). If you have a nice big barn, or a work area where you can hang something heavy from the ceiling, this is not a bad idea at all. Bike mechanics

know that repairing a puncture is an annoying job. It is a well-known secret that bike mechanics would rather not do it and will almost always make up an excuse if they can think of one. If they get the chance, they just throw a new inner tube around your wheel. You can't really blame the bike mechanic for this. Inner tubes cost next to nothing, and if you put one in, you avoid the risk that the customer will be back within an hour 'because it's flat again'.

Repairing a puncture is something that you might traditionally learn from a parent. It is a ritual. There are steps – the importance of which appears to be heavily exaggerated – that you might be tempted to skip. Only to slowly arrive at the conclusion that the steps were less exaggerated than you initially thought.

STEP-BY-STEP INSTRUCTIONS

PUNCTURE REPAIR

TOOLS REQUIRED

Tyre levers   Scissors

Bicycle pump   Abrasive paper

Bucket of water   Talcum powder

Chalk or pen

Patch

Solution

- Turn the bike upside down.

- Remove the dust cap from the valve and loosen the ring on the valve; remove the rubber from the valve and allow the remaining air to escape from the tyre.

- Now loosen the ring that retains the valve. Place the valve components somewhere safe so that you don't lose them.

- Push the bead – the strong iron wire that holds the tyre in the rim – well towards the centre.

- Push the valve inwards as far as possible.

- Push a tyre lever between the outer tyre and the rim, and wedge it firmly behind a spoke.

- Lever one side of the outer tyre over the edge of the rim, using another tyre lever. Now push your tyre levers two spokes further around, until the outer tyre comes completely loose.

- Push the valve through the hole and remove the inner tube from inside the outer tyre.

- Pump up the inner tube.

- Listen for where the hole is. If you don't hear anything, place the inner tube in a bucket of water – you will see bubbles escaping from where the hole is.

STEP-BY-STEP INSTRUCTIONS

PUNCTURE REPAIR (CONTINUED)

- Mark the hole with chalk or a pen. Cut a nice round hole with a pair of small scissors.*

- Roughen the tube around the hole with abrasive paper.

- Smear the solution around it, then wait a few minutes until the solution is dry, until the glue becomes matt (have 'solution patience').

- Press on a nice large patch. If you are using ready-made patches, leave the transparent protective film on there.

- Check your sticking work.

- Check that there are no sharp objects remaining in the inside or outside of the outer tyre.

- Inflate the inner tube (not too hard), to check that the patch has stuck properly.

- Let some air back out of the tyre.

- Sprinkle some talcum powder on the tyre to prevent the inner tube sticking to the outer tyre.

- Place the inner tube back in the outer tyre.

- Place the outer tyre back on the rim. Begin with the side opposite the valve. Do not use a tyre lever!

- Turn the bike the right way up again.

- Pump the tyre back up.

- If the tyre goes flat again after a while, go back to the first step.

*Some bike mechanics cut a round hole around a small split in an inner tube, to prevent the split spreading further.

PUNCTURE REPAIR

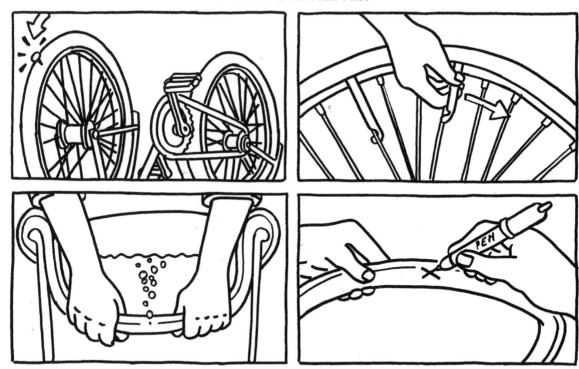

PUNCTURE REPAIR

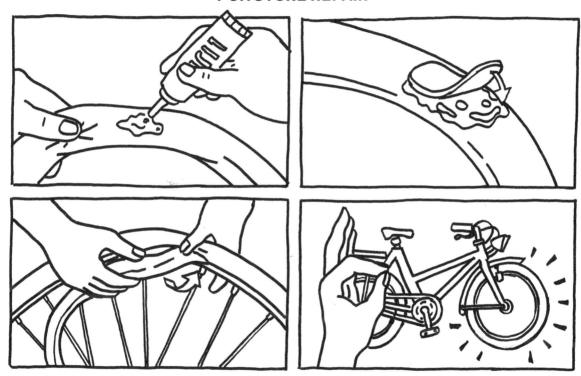

SOLUTION

Solution is a rubber cement tyre adhesive. It consists of rubber granulate that has been diluted (hence the word 'solution') in benzine and toluene. Toluene is the active substance in glue sniffing. It is most definitely not good for you.

LATEX

If you're in the middle of your puncture repair and you can't make the patch stick, there is a drastic remedy. You can buy small bottles of latex, with a pointed spout that you can use to squirt the latex into the valve of the inner tube. The latex will fill the hole from the inside, and you can re-inflate the tyre. Naturally, this doesn't work for large holes and burst tyres.

NEW INNER TUBE

If the hole in the tube is too big, or if there are several holes in the tube, it's better to install a completely new inner tube in the wheel.

VALVE

There are three common valve types. For a regular city bike, this is usually the Woods valve from Dunlop. There are also the French Presta valves and American Schrader valves, which are similar to the valves found on car tyres. Which valve is on a tyre doesn't matter too much, as long as you have the matching bicycle pump. Adapter nipples are available to ensure that you can still pump up a bike tyre that has a different valve.

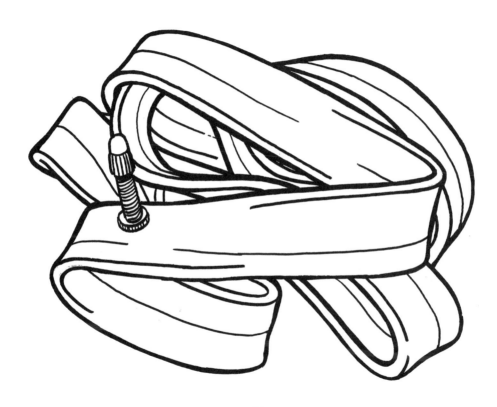

TYRE SIZES

The sizes of bike tyres are maddening. For some reason, the size of a wheel is expressed in inches (1 inch is 2.58 centimetres). For a city bike, you usually need 28-inch tyres. If you see something like **28 X 1⅝ X 1⅜**, this means that the diameter of the outermost edge of the tyre is 28 inches (approximately 72.2 centimetres), the thickness of the tyre is 1⅝ inches, and the width is 1³/₈.

To make things even more confusing, there is also a French size. This states the outer diameter and the width of the tyre and looks like this: **700 X 35C**.

These days, on almost every tyre, you will also find the ETRTO size; for example, **37-622**. This means a tyre that is 37 millimetres (about 1¹/₂ inches) wide, with a diameter of 622 millimetres (about 24¹/₂ inches). Please note that in contrast to the French size, the innermost edge of the tyre is taken to measure the diameter, the so-called bead, an iron wire in the tyre that presses on the rim.

The 37-622 tyre is the usual size for the city bike. A tyre like this should be inflated to 3.5 bar. The Netherlands is also known for its grandma and grandpa bikes, with a tyre size of 40-635. This is a size that you hardly ever encounter anywhere else in Europe or America, but you do find in India and China.

The width of the tyre depends on the space available for the tyre in the frame. A narrower tyre needs to be pumped up harder, whereas a broader tyre can be a little softer, and is a little more suited to a city bike.

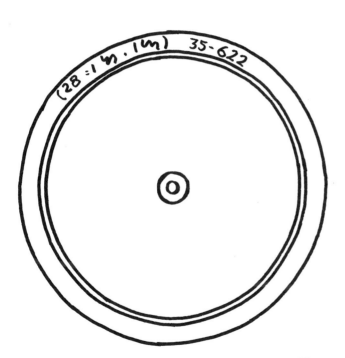

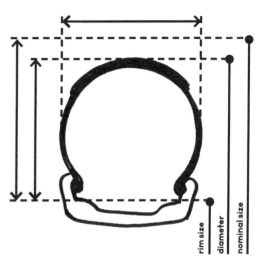

rim size
diameter
nominal size

ARE YOU AFRAID OF SLIDING IN THE WINTER? THERE ARE ALSO WINTER TYRES AVAILABLE FOR BIKES, AND EVEN TYRES WITH SPIKES. YOU CAN ALSO PUT TIE WRAPS AROUND YOUR TYRES, TO CREATE A KIND OF SNOW CHAIN. ALTHOUGH YOU CAN'T DO THIS WITH DISC BRAKES, AS IT WOULD PREVENT YOU BEING ABLE TO BRAKE.

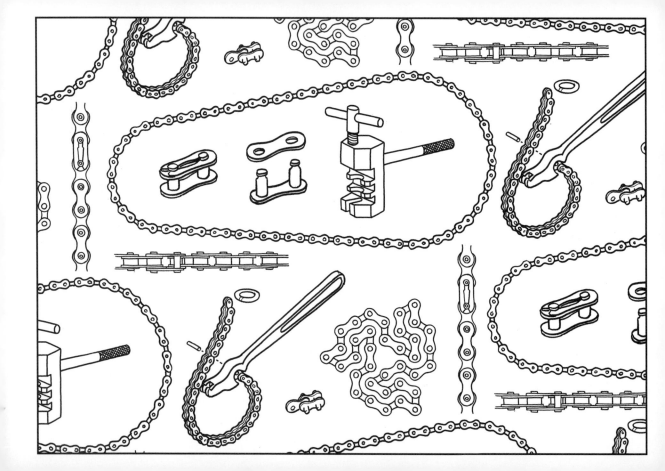

CHAIN

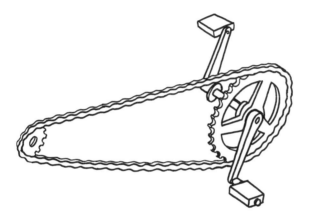

It's happened to everyone at least once: it's windy, it's raining and you want to get home in a hurry, but then... the chain comes off. Curses. Turn the bike over, place the chain back on the gears. Black fingers. Painful hands. With a bit of bad luck you've also cut your hands open.

And just when you're happy with your problem-solving skills, the chain comes off again.

A common cause of the above problem is a worn chain, or a chain that needs adjustment.

STEP-BY-STEP INSTRUCTIONS

ADJUSTING THE CHAIN

1. Free up the chain. Remove any chain guard.

2. Try to move the chain back and forth between the cogs.

3. Slack or play of around a centimetre (¹/₂ inch) is fine. Too little slack is not good.

4. If there is too much slack, loosen the rear wheel nuts.

5. Now loosen the brake assembly.

6. Turn the chain spanners on both sides, until the chain is tight enough.

7. The chain must still have some slack.

Don't have any chain spanners? You can tighten the chain tension by loosening the rear wheel nuts (and if necessary, the brake assembly) and moving the wheel slightly further to the rear, and re-tightening them.

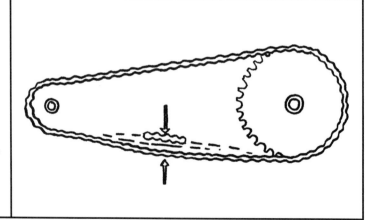

CHAIN GUARD

A chain is often protected in a chain guard, but it doesn't have to be. Without a chain guard, a chain becomes dirty, but if you don't have a derailleur (i.e. if the chain always turns on the same cogs), it isn't such a big problem. Certainly not if you have a stainless steel chain or one that is rust-protected. A new chain can be purchased quite cheaply and is easy to install yourself. However, a chain that is permanently open must be regularly lubricated. Use lubricant that sticks to the chain, which makes it suitable for wet conditions.

A chain guard has two functions: to protect clothing from the dirt of the chain, and to protect the chain from dirt from outside.

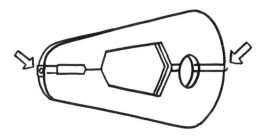

Opening a two-piece chain guard

STEP-BY-STEP INSTRUCTIONS

SHORTENING THE CHAIN

If there is more than a few centimetres of slack, you can shorten the chain slightly using a chain tool.

One of the links has a locking spring. This can be removed, so you can take out a link using the chain tool.

The closed side of the connecting link must be in the chain's direction of travel. If you attach the connecting link the other way around, it may continue to catch somewhere behind.

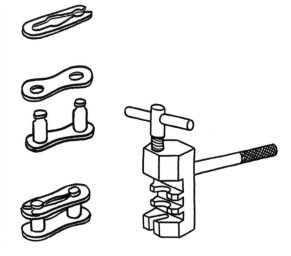

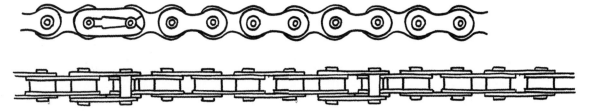

STEP-BY-STEP INSTRUCTIONS

LUBRICATING THE CHAIN

There's no point lubricating a dirty chain, so always clean the chain first.

1. Spray the chain with degreaser or special chain cleaner.

2. Let the chain turn, and dry it with a (lint-free) cloth.

3. If necessary, brush it with a chain brush. This is a brush designed specially for the job.

4. Take a small bottle of chain oil (use oil that is suitable for wet weather).

5. Let the chain turn again and spray the oil onto the inner side of the links.

6. Allow the oil to sink into the chain for a few minutes.

7. Remove any excess lubricant with the cloth.

STEP-BY-STEP INSTRUCTIONS

SLIPPING CHAIN

If the bike's chain is slipping, there could be several reasons:

-   Sometimes the chain is just dirty. The cogs do not grip the chain properly due to the dirt.

-   The chain tension could be too low.

-   The gears could be incorrectly adjusted.

-   The cogs could be worn, so they are not gripping the chain properly.

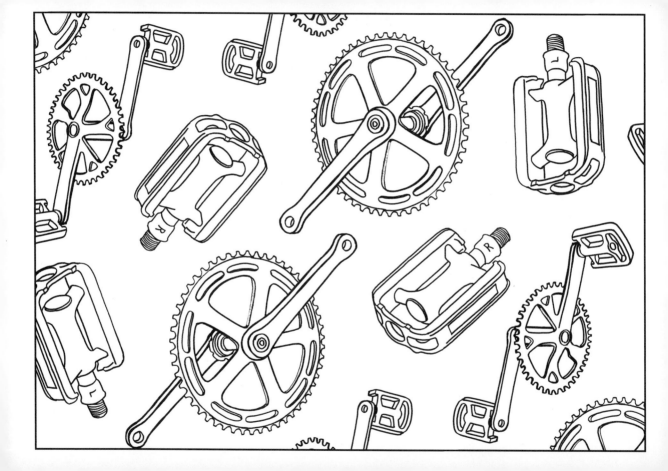

PEDALS

A pedal looks a bit like a hub. It consists of three components: the axle attached to the crank; the rotating platform you put your foot on; and the ball bearings that ensure the pedal can rotate while the axle attaching it to the bike does not rotate around its own axis.

If there are any problems with the pedals, this may be down to a problem with the ball bearings. If the pedals do not rotate straight, the pedals may be bent. In both instances, it is best to replace the pedals.

STEP-BY-STEP INSTRUCTIONS

REPLACING PEDALS

1. The left pedal and right pedal are different. There is a marking on the treadle stating whether a pedal is 'L' or 'R'.

2. Loosening the left pedal is done clockwise, tightening it is anticlockwise. So, exactly the opposite of what you are used to. The various screw threads are there to prevent the pedal from coming loose during cycling. In fact, the opposite happens: the pedal rotates increasingly faster. With older bikes it's not easy to loosen a treadle (and absolutely not if you are turning the wrong way). It can be useful to use a special pedal spanner. This is a long, size-15 spanner which makes it easier to undo the nut.

3. If the pedal still won't loosen, you can place a meter-long iron pipe over the spanner, to give you extra leverage.

4. Turn the new pedal on the crank. A professional would put a small drop of lubricant on the screw thread before screwing the treadle back on. Don't use a spanner to tighten up the first bit, to avoid damaging the screw thread.

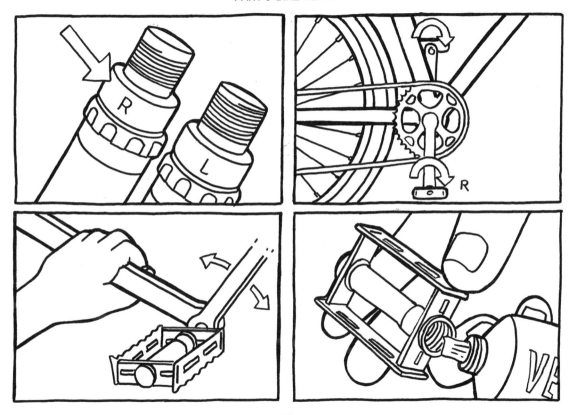

CRANK

The crank is the connecting piece between the bike's bottom bracket and the pedal. Together, the bottom bracket, the cranks and the cog attached to it are called the crank set.

There are generally two types of crank: a crank that is attached with a 'spline' and a splineless crank. The spline is a wedge-shaped piece of metal with a screw thread that ensures that the bottom bracket is attached to the crank. If the crank is in the forward position, the spline must be inserted from top to bottom, with the screw thread end at the bottom.

If there is a little play in the treadles, you can loosen the nut, drive the spline in a little harder using a hammer and re-tighten the nut.

SPLINELESS CRANK

Modern bikes and sports bikes are usually fitted with something called a splineless crank. The bottom bracket ends have a square, conical shape.

STEP-BY-STEP INSTRUCTIONS
REMOVING A SPLINELESS CRANK

1. If necessary, remove the dust cap.

2. Loosen the crank bolt with a narrow socket spanner, the rear of your crank puller tool or, in some cases, a hexagonal wrench. Remove the crank bolt.

3. Now turn the crank puller and turn it as far as possible in the crank.

4. Once the crank puller is fully inserted, turn the centre section inwards, so that the crank is pushed away from the bottom bracket.

STEP-BY-STEP INSTRUCTIONS

FITTING A SPLINELESS CRANK

1. Place the crank on the bottom bracket and drive into place with a synthetic hammer.

2. Screw the crank bolt back into the crank by hand. When it becomes more difficult, use a narrow socket spanner, hexagonal wrench or crank puller, combined with an ordinary spanner. Replace the dust cap.

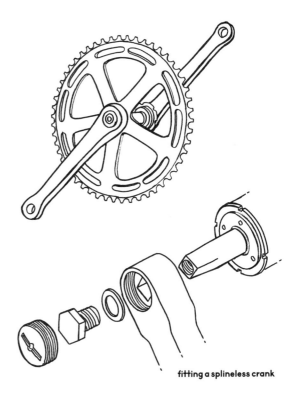

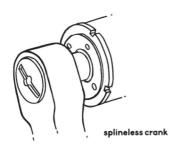

splineless crank

fitting a splineless crank

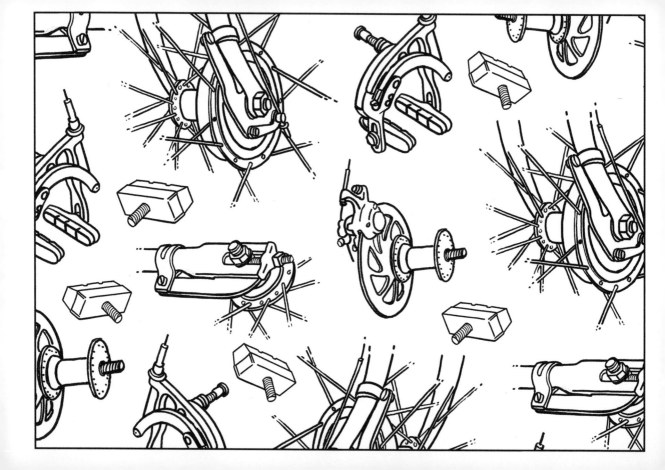

BRAKES

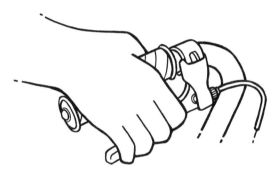

I've had bikes with back-pedal brakes, hand brakes and even one with a drum brake. Because I usually have a shopping bag dangling from the handlebars – I know, not sensible – I prefer the back-pedal brake. With hand braking, one of the brakes always seems to be not quite right. Also, braking with just your front wheel is difficult, and at high speed even a bit dangerous, whereas with a back-pedal brake, you can only brake with your rear wheel. For one reason or another, I used to be too lazy to adjust my hand brakes properly, which is a bit stupid, because it's easier than you think.

81

Rim brakes are easy to adjust. If you can press the brake levers easily as far as the handlebar grips, the tension is too low. You can increase the tension by loosening the brake cable, pulling it tighter and re-tightening the nut. You sometimes have to try a few times to achieve the right tension. You can use the adjustment screw next to the brake lever to adjust it. Turn it outwards to reduce the tension on the cable; turn it inwards to increase the tension.

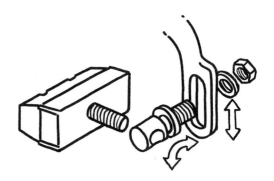

Worn brake blocks must be replaced. This is a very simple rule.

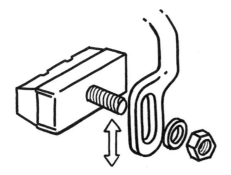

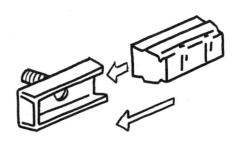

STEP-BY-STEP INSTRUCTIONS

ADJUSTING DISC BRAKES

1. The brake blocks are attached to the holder by a nut that you can loosen with a spanner.

2. 'Relax' the brake by loosening the brake cable.

3. Screw the new blocks into the holder (ensure they are at the correct height) and re-attach the brake cable.

With newer bikes, you can loosen and tighten the brake blocks with hexagonal wrenches and they can be replaced together with the holder. You can adjust the brake blocks by moving them closer to and further away from the rim with a screw.

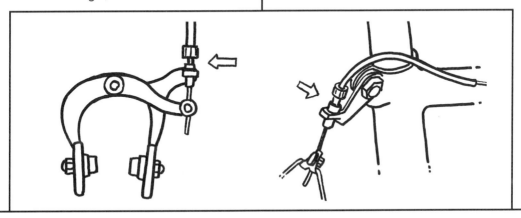

LOCKS

As I said at the beginning, I never used to appreciate my bikes. I never looked after them properly, and I paid very little attention to the unique components that even an ordinary bone-shaker has. The cause was probably fear of commitment. You should not become attached to your bike. Sooner or later bikes get stolen. Unless you are very good with locks... then you can allow yourself to become attached to your bike.

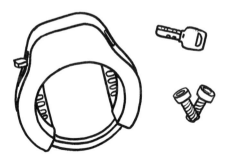

STEP-BY-STEP INSTRUCTIONS
FITTING A RING LOCK

Ring locks are easy to use, because they are attached to your bike.

1. Attach the ring lock with two socket-head screws.

2. Don't tighten the bolts too tightly, as this can make the lock difficult to close.

3. Check that the lock doesn't rattle and opens and closes easily.

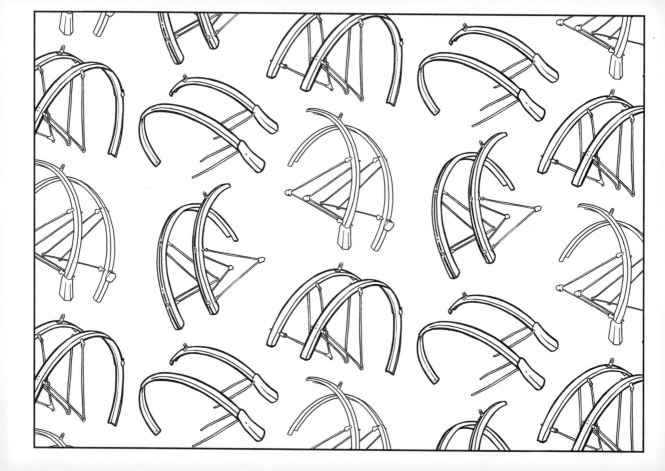

MUDGUARD

attaching a mudguard

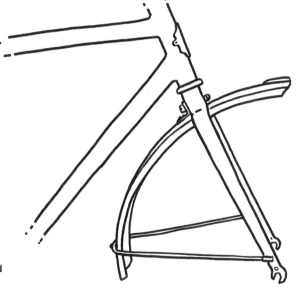

A rattling mudguard is often the result of a mudguard that has rusted through. Unscrew the old one and replace it with a new one.

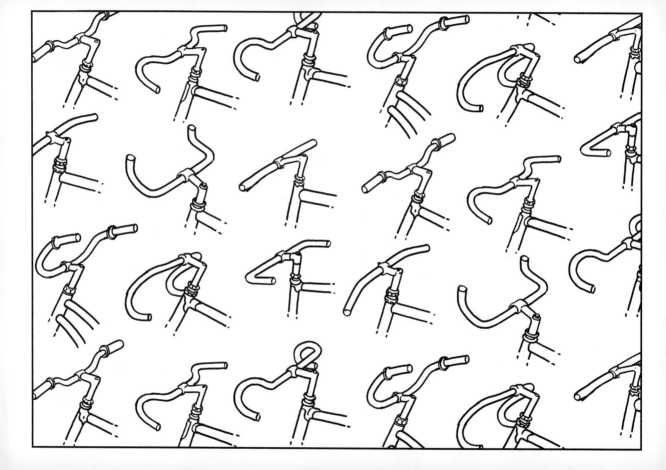

HANDLEBARS

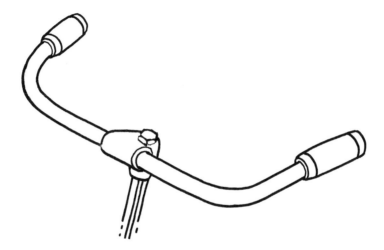

As I said earlier, handlebars are not simply a brace to use for steering. The interaction between the handlebars and frame makes a bike stable.

So stable that you could give most bikes a push and they would remain travelling upright for a few seconds without a rider sitting on them.

Bike handlebars consist of a handlebar stem and the handlebars themselves: the brace to which the hand grips are attached.

HANDLEBAR STEM

The handlebar stem is a hollow tube that fits in the head tube, which is attached to the front fork. Running through the hollow handlebar stem is the expander, a rod with an 'expander cone' at the bottom and an 'expander bolt' at the top. Turning the bolt expands the cone and fixes the handlebars in place.

STEP-BY-STEP INSTRUCTIONS

RAISING OR LOWERING THE STEM

1. Loosen the expander bolt.

2. Give the bolt a tap with a synthetic hammer, so that the bolt can now move back and forth.

3. Clamp the front wheel between your legs and set the handlebars to the correct height by moving them back and forth. Tighten up the expander bolt once more.

HEADSET

The headset is the part of the handlebars that transmits the steering movement to the front forks. It is a small cylinder made up of rings and nuts. Removing the headset reveals two ball bearings. These ball bearings have a lot to withstand and can be replaced if they are worn.

If you move your handlebars up and down using the hand grips, there should be no play in the headset. To resolve any play, you can loosen the uppermost nut – the 'headset nut' – a little with a spanner. You can then turn the ring beneath it slightly until the play disappears.

REPLACING HAND GRIPS

Bike hand grips are sometimes attached very firmly. If you want to replace them, you can slip a screwdriver under each grip and squirt a bit of lubricant underneath, so that the grip slides off more easily.

When you put new hand grips on your handlebars, you must first clean the handlebars thoroughly. You can then dampen the handlebars so that the grips slide on more easily. White spirit is also suitable for this. You must never use lubricant for the new grips, as this makes the handlebars slippery.

BELL

The bell usually sits on the left side of the handlebars. This dates from the times when bikes had horns – you could keep your dominant hand on the handlebars and use the horn with your left hand. Bells have been compulsory since 1906. And that's good, because you've now maintained your bike so well that it hardly makes a sound.

LIGHTS

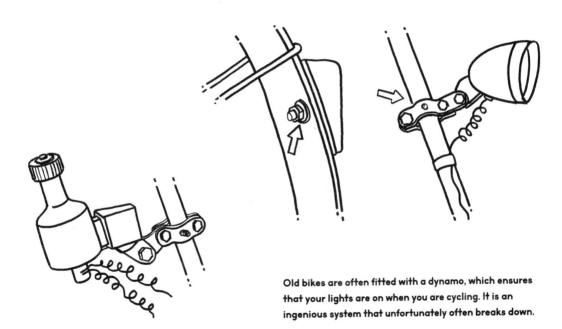

Old bikes are often fitted with a dynamo, which ensures that your lights are on when you are cycling. It is an ingenious system that unfortunately often breaks down.

STEP-BY-STEP INSTRUCTIONS

REPAIRING BIKE LIGHTS

IS THE FRONT OR REAR LIGHT NOT WORKING?

1. Is the dynamo working, but the front or rear light isn't? Replace the bulb.

2. Still not working? Check whether a wire has become loose.

DO BOTH THE FRONT AND REAR LIGHTS NOT WORK?

1. Check that the impeller is still touching the tyre correctly.

2. Check the wiring.

3. If the dynamo is rusty or broken, replace it, or change to lights that run on batteries.

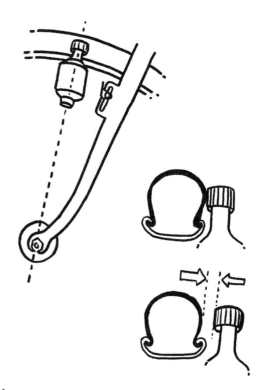

BATTERY LIGHTS

The best rear light is an LED light that runs on AA batteries. It can last an entire winter, as long as it is not stolen from your bike. A front light is brighter and requires more energy, so it needs new batteries more often.

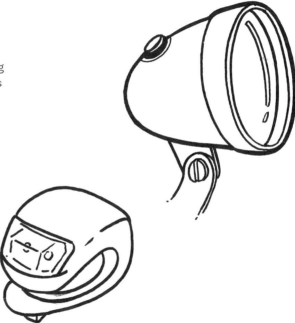

GEARS

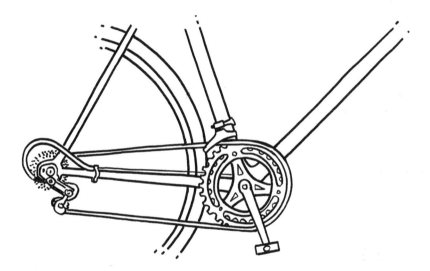

Whenever I had a bike with gears, I found that the pedals would suddenly slip, or the bike would unexpectedly change from one gear to another.

Sometimes I only had third gear, and other times only first. Ridiculous! Because it's unbelievably easy to adjust the gears yourself.

There is only one rule when adjusting gears: pull the cable 'hand tight' when it is in its most relaxed position. This usually gives you the correct cable tension.

STURMEY ARCHER 3

You can screw the gear cable tight with a bolt which sits in a small chain attached to a pin that is threaded into the rear wheel hub on the other side.

If it is in second gear, and you look through the hole in the nut (see below), the lever must just disappear from your view. You can control this by pulling the gear cable tighter or looser.

MODERN HUB GEARS

With modern hub gears, such as those from Shimano, you can adjust the gears by turning a nut or an adjustment screw, as long as the stripes on the gear housing are in line with the rear hub. With the Shimano Nexus 3, the stripes must be the same as those in second gear. With the Shimano 7/8, this applies to fourth gear.

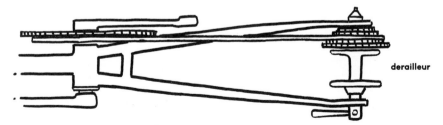

derailleur

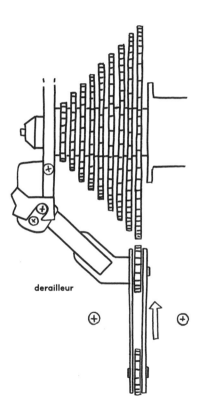

derailleur

DERAILLEUR

If you have a bike with a derailleur, you can adjust the gears using two adjustment screws and the adjustment screw for the cable tension.

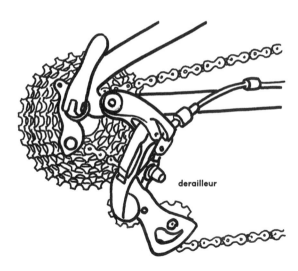

derailleur

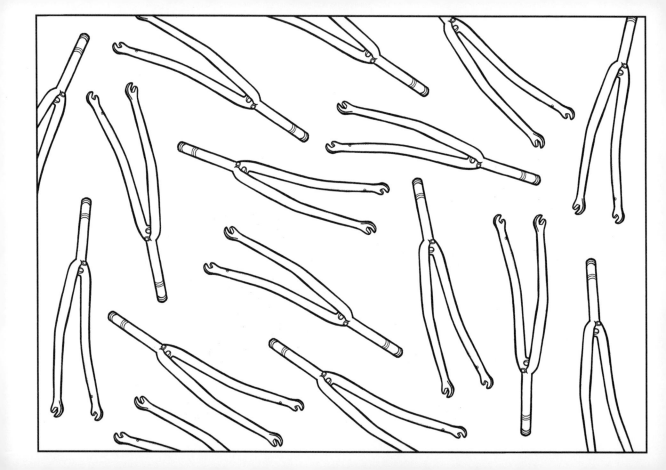

FRONT FORK

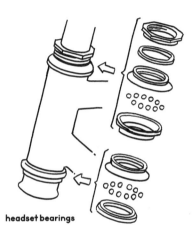

headset bearings

The position of the two fork blades in relation to each other and to the head tube is important. They must not be too warped. Are they warped? If so, you can try to bend them slightly, but in some cases it might be better to go to the bike mechanic.

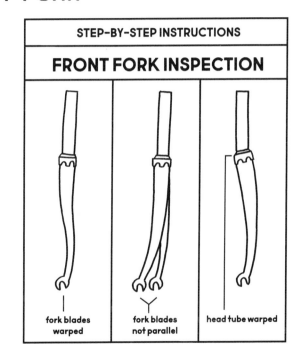

STEP-BY-STEP INSTRUCTIONS

FRONT FORK INSPECTION

fork blades warped

fork blades not parallel

head tube warped

WHEEL

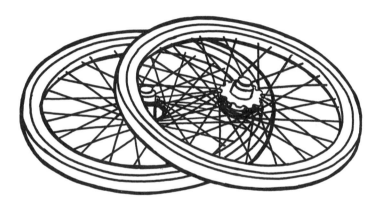

A broken spoke doesn't seem that serious. There are enough spokes in a wheel. Aren't there? No, not really. Other spokes will break more quickly if one spoke is already broken. It's always a good idea to replace a broken spoke.

STEP-BY-STEP INSTRUCTIONS

REPLACING A SPOKE

1. Remove the wheel from the bike.

2. Loosen the spoke nipple on the rim (if that is still necessary) and remove the broken spoke.

3. Insert the new spoke (of the correct length and thickness).

4. Lace the spoke in the same way as a similar spoke and tighten in the nipple.

5. Tighten the spoke with a spoke spanner.

REPLACE THE NIPPLE

If the spoke is loose in the nipple, you also need to replace the nipple. To do this you must first slide the outer tyre to one side and lift up the rim tape to be able to remove the nipple.

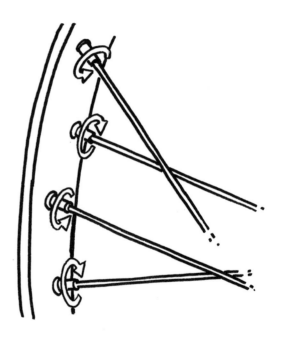

HOW TO REMOVE A BUCKLE FROM YOUR WHEEL

A buckle in your wheel is almost impossible to avoid if you have a city lifestyle. Bikes placed in bike racks are not always handled with silk gloves. If a buckle in a wheel is so bad that it prevents you from cycling, there is a drastic remedy. And that's simply to jump on the wheel, for just as long as you need to until it can be ridden again. Although this means you can ride the bike again, your wheel will never be the same. And sooner or later, you will have problems with spokes coming loose or your bike becoming more difficult to pedal.

If the rim is not badly buckled, there are several more elegant ways to solve the problem. For a small buckle in the wheel, you can adjust the spoke tension so that the buckle disappears. But you do need a wheel straightener for this (see page 47).

A wheel straightener allows you to determine where the buckle in the wheel is located. You can repair a small buckle by tightening the spokes on one side and slightly loosening them on the other side. You will need a spoke spanner for this (see page 38). The direction in which you tighten them is exactly the opposite to what you would expect, unless you expect something other than what most people would expect.

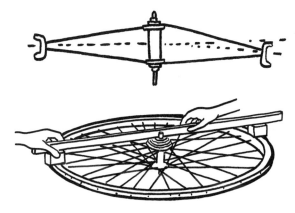

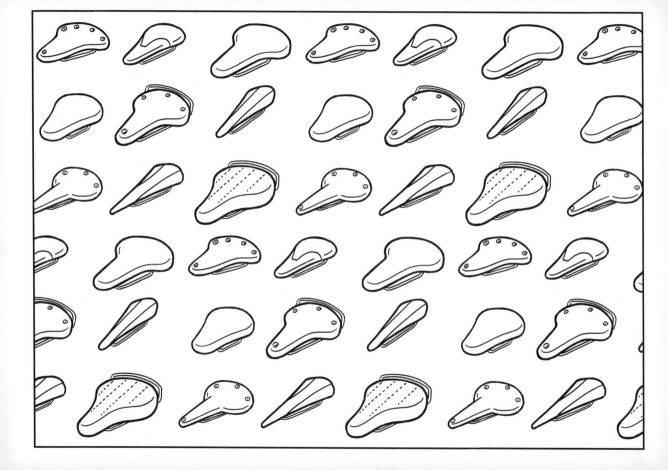

SADDLE

I have ridden for hundreds of hours on bikes with loose saddles. Or on a broken saddle that would absorb all the moisture from rain showers, so I always had wet trousers. Or a saddle that was slightly too high or too low. Or that would move backwards and forwards, so that I would almost slide off it. I only ever thought about it when I got back on the bike, and was usually too lazy to go looking for an ordinary spanner or a hexagonal wrench. Stupid, as the replacement or adjustment of a saddle is a very simple job.

STEP-BY-STEP INSTRUCTIONS

REPOSITIONING/REPLACING THE SADDLE

Try to loosen the saddle strap with a number 13 or 14 spanner. You can now remove the saddle to adjust or replace it, as you wish. Then tighten it up again with the spanner.

On newer bikes, the saddle and saddle strap are integrated. To loosen these, you will need a hexagonal wrench.

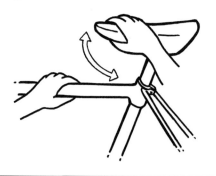

SADDLE SORENESS

Saddle soreness is unpleasant, but it's not just about the saddle – weight and the position on the bike also have an effect.

The perfect saddle is different for everybody; it depends on a person's sit bones, the two lowest protuberances of the pelvic bone. The distance between the sit bones varies slightly for everyone, and so the width of the ideal saddle varies too. If you suffer badly from saddle soreness, you can have this distance measured at a bike shop, so you can find out the correct width of your perfect saddle.

If you are well-supported on your sit bones, you suffer less from saddle soreness. Soft gel saddles appear to be a good solution, but they aren't, because the sit bones sink into them and can't find proper support. If you want to get rid of saddle soreness, in fact you need a harder saddle, with a width that fits you.

ADJUSTING THE SADDLE

The distance from the saddle to the pedals is important. If the saddle is too low, you can't use enough force and you place too much load on your knees. If the saddle is too high, you 'overstretch' your legs and you move back and forth. Your knee should be not quite stretched out when you press the pedal completely down. You can calculate the correct height using your inside leg measurement. This is the length from your feet to your groin, on the inner side of your legs.

The frame size is the distance from the centre of the bottom bracket to the place in the frame where the saddle goes. The frame size itself should be approximately two-thirds of your inside leg length. So, if your inside leg measurement is 90 cm (35 in), a frame size of 60 cm (23 in) is perfect.

The rule of thumb for the distance of your saddle to the bottom bracket is that it should be 0.92 of your inside leg measurement. Personally, I prefer my saddle to be a bit lower, so I can stand with my feet on the ground very easily. But I wouldn't say that out loud to a bike mechanic or enthusiast.

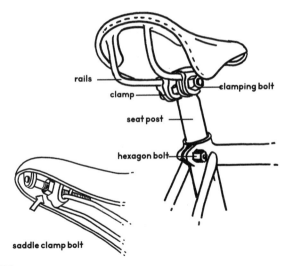

rails
clamp
clamping bolt
seat post
hexagon bolt
saddle clamp bolt

SAFE BIKE

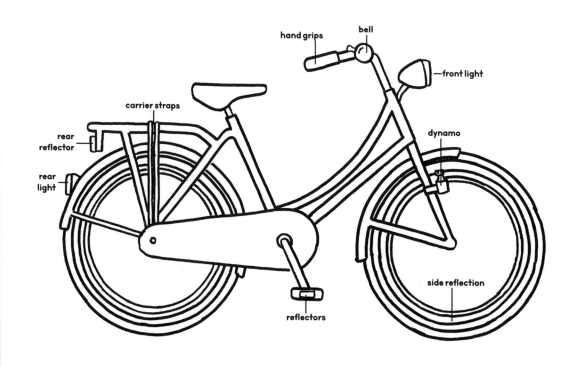

hand grips

bell

front light

carrier straps

dynamo

rear reflector

rear light

side reflection

reflectors

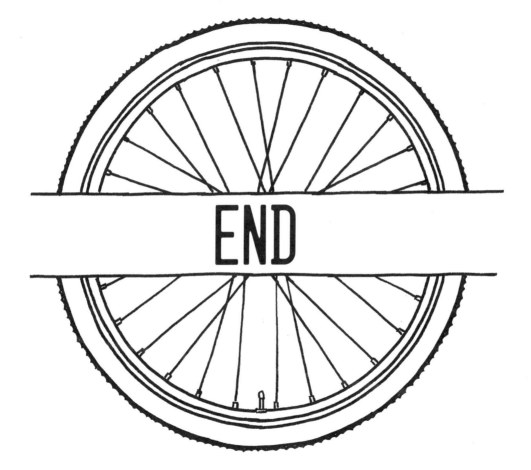

END

First published in 2020 by Snor

This English language hardback edition published in 2021 by Quadrille

The rights to this book were negotiated through Sea of Stories Literary Agency, www.seaofstories.com, sidonie@seaofstories.com.

First published in 2021 by Quadrille, an imprint
of Hardie Grant Publishing
52–54 Southwark Street
London SE1 1UN
quadrille.com

For the English language hardback edition:
PUBLISHING DIRECTOR Sarah Lavelle
EDITOR Stacey Cleworth
JUNIOR DESIGNER Alicia House
HEAD OF PRODUCTION Stephen Lang
SENIOR PRODUCTION CONTROLLER Katie Jarvis

Cataloguing in Publication Data: a catalogue record for this book is available from the British Library.

Text © Gerard Janssen 2021
Illustration and design © Studio Boot 2021
Layout © Quadrille 2021

ISBN 978 1 78713 688 5
Printed in China